A PERFECT FUTURE

David Hay

BROADWAY PLAY PUBLISHING INC
224 E 62nd St, NY, NY 10065
www.broadwayplaypub.com
info@broadwayplaypub.com

A PERFECT FUTURE
© Copyright 2011 by David Hay

First printing: December 2011
Second printing: February 2012
I S B N: 978-0-88145-513-7

Book design: Marie Donovan
Page make-up: Adobe Indesign
Typeface: Palatino
Printed and bound in the U S A

The world premiere of A PERFECT FUTURE opened at the Cherry Lane Theater in New York City on 17 February 2011. It was produced by Andy Sandberg with Whitney Hoagland Edwards and Neal-Rose Creations. The cast and creative contributors were:

NATALIE SCHIFF-HUDSON .... Donna Bullock
ELLIOT MURPHY .... Daniel Oreskes
JOHN HUDSON .... Michael T Weiss
MARK COLVIN .... Scott Drummond

Director .... Wilson Milam
Set design .... Charlie Corcoran
Costume design .... Michael McDonald
Lighting design .... Ben Stanton
Sound design .... Daniel Kluger
General manager .... Denise Cooper
Casting .... Pat McCorkle
Production stage manager .... Donald Fried
Assistant stage manager .... Melissa Jernigan

The play was developed in association with Naked Angels.

CHARACTERS & SETTING

NATALIE SCHIFF-HUDSON, *a documentary filmmaker in her mid-50s*

ELLIOT MURPHY, *the same age, he's an officer in an AIDS organization on Los Angeles*

JOHN HUDSON, *the same generation as his wife,* NATALIE, *and* ELLIOT, *he operates in the upper echelons of the finance world*

MARK COLVIN, *30 years old, and undeniably corporate*

A living room in a large New York apartment belonging to a well-to-do couple. An archway leads to an entrance hall. There are copious bookshelves and two small doors, one on each side of the room.

Time: The Fall of 2005

ACT ONE

(In the hallway)

NATALIE: We did, we did!

ELLIOT: Of course we did!

(NATALIE SCHIFF-HUDSON, carrying a dish towel, enters followed by ELLIOT MURPHY.)

NATALIE: All of us on our knees in the living room? Snorting lines off the coffee table? We couldn't see a Bertolucci movie unless we were high.

ELLIOT: John certainly couldn't.

NATALIE: Not our John. God, no... As soon as we squeezed into the Volvo, he had to run back inside and snort between the cracks for leftovers.

ELLIOT: Didn't we drive off without him?

NATALIE: Oh my God, did we? Who was driving?

ELLIOT: God, I miss cocaine. You sure you don't have some on hand?

NATALIE: Elliot.

ELLIOT: Just asking.

(NATALIE picks up a glass that has been sitting on a side table along with a just-opened bottle of wine.)

NATALIE: You're just going to have to settle for something from John's wine collection. He has a sommelier now...

ELLIOT: He does?

NATALIE: A good one actually. He's supposed to be very savvy. *(She looks at the label.)*

NATALIE: This is from Oregon. They talk about it all the time. *(She pours him a glass.)* I can't believe you don't remember going to *Last Tango*...

ELLIOT: I remember John being obsessed with her boobs... What was her name?

NATALIE: Maria Schneider.

ELLIOT: Of course. Maria Schneider.

NATALIE: You can bet John hasn't forgotten.

ELLIOT: What about the butter?

NATALIE: Oh my God, the butter! The butter! Well, he was forty-nine...So, tell me, please, the committee: how is Muhammad?

ELLIOT: Natalie, they showed me the police reports. You'd have to be a genius to make a bomb out of what the F B I "found" in his apartment. It's a total set-up. They re-invented him as a domestic terrorist to justify everything they're doing to this country.

NATALIE: I heard he was perfectly happy running those free clinics he started.

ELLIOT: He was a Panther, Natalie. They don't forget.

NATALIE: I know.

ELLIOT: I saw him last year. Did I tell you?

NATALIE: No.

ELLIOT: I was at this community health conference in Tuscaloosa.

NATALIE: Did you talk?

ELLIOT: I'm there—packed into this ugly ballroom— and this large black guy gets up and starts going off about "the imperialism of the healthcare industry" and "genocide by lack of health benefits". I thought, "Who is that guy with the white afro making so much sense"? It was Muhammad.

NATALIE: You said "hello", I hope?

ELLIOT: Of course. We talked about my AIDS work. His Community Clinics. He just opened one in Panama City, you know.

NATALIE: Didn't you talk about us? You must've?

ELLIOT: His clinic manager was there.

NATALIE: Some young thing?

ELLIOT: A very serious black man. You want to know something? This is the best thing I've done in years.

NATALIE: What are you talking about? You have an important job.

ELLIOT: I'm hardly on the front lines.

NATALIE: Of course you are.

ELLIOT: It's so far from when I started. Back in the days when we were rushing people to the emergency room. Smuggling the latest "wonder drug" in from Mexico. Sit-ins at the N I H... Now when I go into work I get to confront issues like—what's allowed on your desk. Photos have to be in picture frames. No naked men. No naked men? How in the hell do they think AIDS started? Jesus...I don't care. The moment they called to ask if I wanted to help Muhammad, I was my old self again. The raving political lunatic...well, wannabe raving political lunatic. *(Off wine)* This is good. You're not having any?

NATALIE: John says the real, die-hard aficionados insist on taking a month off. Every now and then. To revive the palette. I'm giving it a try.

ELLIOT: You're sure about that?

(ELLIOT *offers* NATALIE *his glass, but she waves it off.*)

NATALIE: We'll give you whatever you need, don't worry. I wish we could do more.

ELLIOT: I'd love you to join the committee, Natalie.

NATALIE: Elliot, I'm in New York.

ELLIOT: So what? Fly out to L A for meetings.

NATALIE: I can't.

ELLIOT: We need you. I need you. It's Muhammad. Muhammad from our *Kapital* reading group.

NATALIE: God...the *Kapital* reading group.

ELLIOT: I think I'm the only one who actually got through all three volumes.

NATALIE: John did. John always says the reason he's made it to the top is Karl Marx.

ELLIOT: Well, I know you didn't get past *The Communist Manifesto*.

NATALIE: I was there for the sex. Like you. Admit it. (*She opens one of the small doors. In a hallway behind are some old cardboard boxes. She starts rifling through them.*)

ELLIOT: Natalie!

NATALIE: Well, you were!

ELLIOT: You need to be on the committee, Mrs Hudson.

NATALIE: Mrs Schiff-Hudson to you.

ELLIOT: What are you doing?

NATALIE: Just a minute. Found it!

(NATALIE *returns to the living room holding her three volumes of* Das Kapital *from college. She tosses them to* ELLIOT.)

NATALIE: Here!

ELLIOT: *(Catching them)* You're kidding! You still have this?

NATALIE: I hope you're hungry. We're having John's favorite meal.

ELLIOT: Great. *(Intrigued by the volumes of* Das Kapital, *he sits down with them.)*

NATALIE: Let's hope so. John's quite particular. I'm sure it'll all be fine...I never used to worry about dinner parties, did I? Back on Shattuck. What's happened to me?

ELLIOT: *(Looking up)* I don't recall us ever quite making it to "dinner parties". All I remember were endless, stoned affairs. Everything emptied out of the fridge and tossed into the wok.

NATALIE: The wok! The wok! I loved the wok!

ELLIOT: "The wok: the ultimate non-discriminatory utensil. Likes everything. Brown rice. Scallions."

NATALIE: Tuna, beans, daffodils...

ELLIOT: Yeast, compost...

NATALIE: Elliot, stop... Stop. I won't have you disrespecting the wok. We lived out of that thing.

ELLIOT: We did, didn't we?

NATALIE: Until you forced us to get that cookbook.

ELLIOT: What cook book?

NATALIE: *The Vegetarian Epicure.*

ELLIOT: Oh, Jesus, don't bring that up.

NATALIE: I still have it. Up here somewhere. *(She gets up and surveys the bookshelves.)*

ELLIOT: God, whoever wrote that must've been shitting brown rice all day long.

NATALIE: And remember the farts?

ELLIOT: God, Natalie, no...

NATALIE: God, Natalie, yes.

ELLIOT: We were all so high all the time. Are you sure you don't have any coke?

NATALIE: I should have ordered some in.

ELLIOT: You used to keep a stash in the editing room.

NATALIE: I did, didn't I?

ELLIOT: I'm sorry. I'm so sorry. I haven't even asked. The movie? How is it?

NATALIE: Elliot.

ELLIOT: What?

NATALIE: Subject off-limits. Sorry, sweetie... If you must know, I'm having an impossible time. All this footage and...nothing.

ELLIOT: I don't understand. You're the best.

NATALIE: I was.

ELLIOT: You are. Cinema as a gun.

NATALIE: I miss 16 millimeter. I still have my original Éclair, you know. Everyone'd think it was a relic if they saw it. But there was something about those images. They had authenticity. That's the problem with Hi-Def. Everything ends up looking so pristine, artificial...This is Rwanda, not Disneyland.

ELLIOT: I'm sure it's brilliant as it always is.

NATALIE: The real problem was... was getting them to be honest. We spent weeks in those camps trying to earn their trust. Persuading them we could actually be of some help. But all they wanted was—

ELLIOT: ...food and water.

NATALIE: Yes, and after that C Ds and T-shirts. If we'd been able to give them cell phones, they would have looked into that camera and said anything. Even how grateful they were to America for letting them starve to death... Surprise, surprise, the footage looks phony. It's not their story.

ELLIOT: I'm sure you're exaggerating.

NATALIE: You know what? Screw John and his wine snobs. I've never actually seen any of them take a day off.

ELLIOT: I never have.

(NATALIE *gets the other glass from the side table and pours herself some of the Oregon wine.* ELLIOT *seizes this chance to glance through* Das Kapital. *She holds up her glass.*)

NATALIE: Cheers.

ELLIOT: Cheers.

(ELLIOT *and* NATALIE *drink. He continues leafing through* Das Kapital.)

ELLIOT: Natalie!

NATALIE: What?

ELLIOT: *Das Kapital!* (*He removes a dried marijuana stem that's been used as a bookmark and holds it up.*) Is that what I think it is?

(NATALIE *sniffs the stem.*)

NATALIE: Sensimilla!

ELLIOT: No, Acapulco Gold!

NATALIE: Hmmm. Humboldt County.

ELLIOT: Maui Zowie.

NATALIE: Maui Zowie!

ELLIOT: Maui Zowie!

(JOHN HUDSON, *the same age and suited as befits a man of high finance, enters. He and* ELLIOT *hug warmly.*)

JOHN: Elliot...buddy.

ELLIOT: John.

NATALIE: He never changes, does he? Looks and talks exactly the same.

JOHN: You look great.

ELLIOT: So do you. What's your secret, that's what I want to know.

JOHN: One of these days I'll tell you.

ELLIOT: We used to look like we were the same age.

JOHN: Back in the days when you were straight.

ELLIOT: In the closet and secretly...desperately trying to convert you.

JOHN: If you'd told me it was the secret to eternal youth...

ELLIOT: "It?"

JOHN: "It."

ELLIOT: God, I wish "it" was.

NATALIE: I want to have surgery. But John won't let me.

JOHN: I love her the way she is. What can I say? I always have.

(JOHN *kisses* NATALIE.)

NATALIE: Now you're embarrassing me.

JOHN: I can say that in front of Elliot.

ELLIOT: You can say anything and everything in front of me.

NATALIE: He says it's decadent.

JOHN: Don't get me wrong. I want us all to be decadent. You especially, Elliot. But we don't need surgery to be decadent.

NATALIE: Elliot was hoping we'd have cocaine.

ELLIOT: Do you?

JOHN: I have better than that.

ELLIOT: I want it.

(JOHN *heads to a door on the other side of the room.*)

NATALIE: I told him we had a sommelier.

JOHN: You laughed, didn't you? ...Well, you should see what he comes up with. (*He opens the door to reveal a cabinet full of well-stocked racks that hold the bottles from his wine collection. Everything is there, including glasses of all types.*)

ELLIOT: Very nice! ...How is he with illegal drugs?

JOHN: He's married with three kids.

ELLIOT: He's straight? John, who's ever heard of a straight sommelier?

NATALIE: You have now.

ELLIOT: Just my luck.

JOHN: Here we are. (*He pulls out a bottle.*) Louis Jadot. Gevrey-Chambertin, 1996. A so-called "essential Burgundy". This'll teach that Oregon Pinot a thing or two... (*He opens the wine.*) Honey, you remembered the fennel?

ELLIOT: Fennel?

NATALIE: In the kitchen.

ELLIOT: What are we having?

NATALIE: Elliot, all good meals are supposed to come with an element of surprise.

JOHN: Yes, they should.

NATALIE: That's what John says.

JJOHN: Yes, I do.

NATALIE: I'm going to have some... I've broken my vow of abstinence.

JOHN: I saw that. (*He gets a third wine glass.*) So, Elliot, what's the occasion? What brings you to New York?

NATALIE: Elliot's on Muhammad's support committee. They want us to help.

JOHN: We saw it on the news.

NATALIE: It was degrading. Truly degrading. Shackled, in that orange jump suit. Dragged into the S U V like...

ELLIOT: Like a slave. That's what it looked like.

NATALIE: I haven't been that upset in... What is it with this country?

JOHN: We'll do right by him, don't you worry.

NATALIE: That's what I told him.

ELLIOT: Thank you. Thank you both. It'll mean a lot. You know that.

NATALIE: That's what we do now. Write checks.

ELLIOT: And thank God you do.

NATALIE: Iraq war veterans, Planned Parenthood. Full page advertisements in *The Times*...Katrina. Katrina...

JOHN: We're doing everything we can... It's good, isn't't?

ELLIOT: More than good...

JOHN: And there's plenty more in case the L S D doesn't arrive.

ELLIOT: I said Natalie should come on the committee. Both of you should.

JOHN: (*To* NATALIE) Why don't you?

NATALIE: I don't want to fly three thousand miles to argue politics with a bunch of blowhards.

ELLIOT: Blowhards?

NATALIE: I want to be in the trenches... Like we used to be. Laying down on the Bay Bridge. Twenty-four hour watch outside Soledad. When your body's on the line, you feel so much more effective.

JOHN: Because that's when the sex happens.

NATALIE: John.

JOHN: What about the Kapital Reading Group?

NATALIE: We were just talking about that.

JOHN: I couldn't keep my eyes off her. I didn't care how much we went on about "commodity exchange value".

NATALIE: I didn't either.

ELLIOT: *(Clearing throat)* Guys.

NATALIE: Elliot, we had sex once.

JOHN: You did?

ELLIOT: Sort of...

NATALIE: He has really sensitive nipples.

ELLIOT: Natalie.

NATALIE: Don't try and deny it.

JOHN: I always wondered why you went gay.

ELLIOT: You should thank me for sending her back to you.

JOHN: You're right. Thank you, Elliot.

ELLIOT: He and I played around a few times.

JOHN: We did?

ELLIOT: In Ensenada. After Hussongs. And I don't know how many margaritas.

NATALIE: Did you touch his nipples?

ELLIOT: We were really drunk.

JOHN: I remember nothing.

ELLIOT: I sucked you off.

JOHN: You did?

ELLIOT: Yes!

JOHN: I thought it was the other way around.

ELLIOT: No, you wish.

JOHN: Well, thank you, Elliot. I hope I thanked you at the time.

ELLIOT: He's coming on to me.

JOHN: More Louis Jadot!

NATALIE: Honey, that'd be perfect for dinner parties. It is a conversation stopper.

JOHN: She's right. The "I've met two Popes" is getting a little stale. "I sucked a man's dick once" has a nice ring to it... Although...how about: "You know I've met two Popes, and sucked *both* their dicks..." What the church doesn't tell you is—those numbers after the names?

ELLIOT: John.

JOHN: You wonder why John the Twenty-third was so popular?

NATALIE: Stop.

JOHN: Here, Elliot... Cheers.

NATALIE: Cheers.

(They toast.)

ELLIOT: You two were legendary.

NATALIE: "Legendary"? For God's sake.

ELLIOT: What?

NATALIE: You make it sound as though we're dead... "There go the sexual legends."

JOHN: "Natalie and John. Screwed themselves to death before Social Security even kicked in."

NATALIE: "Overdosed on Viagra we heard."

ELLIOT: You should be glad you have a sex life.

NATALIE: You're the one with the sex life.

ELLIOT: Hardly.

NATALIE: Oh, c'mon now.

ELLIOT: Those days are long gone.

JOHN: I don't believe that for one minute.

NATALIE: John?

JOHN: Honey?

NATALIE: When was the last time he brought someone here?

ELLIOT: Oh, guys please.

NATALIE: We're at that age when you really need someone.

JOHN: She's right.

ELLIOT: Thank you.

NATALIE: How long have you been single?

ELLIOT: Ten... Fourteen... Sixteen years.

JOHN: You're an eligible guy, Elliot.

NATALIE: What about the committee? There must be someone there?

ELLIOT: Besides the black homophobes and armed struggle advocates?

NATALIE: One step at a time.

JOHN: There is nothing wrong with a good "armed struggle" advocate.

ELLIOT: I'm planning on starting with the sommelier.

NATALIE: He has kids!

ELLIOT: That's what they all say.

(The buzzer sounds.)

JOHN: Oh, shit.

NATALIE: What?

JOHN: We may have an extra guest.

NATALIE: Oh, John.

ELLIOT: What's he talking about?

(JOHN goes into the hall.)

JOHN: *(Off stage)* Yes... Send him up... Thanks, Victor. *(He returns to the room.)*

JOHN: One of my junior associates. Bright guy actually. We were leaving the office and he looked totally down. I invited him over without thinking.

NATALIE: And John thought you might like him.

JOHN: Natalie.

ELLIOT: You're kidding, aren't you?

JOHN: Look, I'm sorry if...

ELLIOT: You haven't changed one bit, have you?

NATALIE: He's probably too young.

ELLIOT: What?

JOHN: Elliot, one drink and I'll send him on his way.

NATALIE: Would you? I'm not sure I'm in the mood for a complete stranger.

(The doorbell sounds.)

JOHN: Okay, okay, guys...I get the message. One drink. *(He exits.)*

ELLIOT: I'm fifty-five, Natalie.

NATALIE: I'm sorry.

ELLIOT: He'd better like wine.

NATALIE: He'll be on his best behavior. He's with the boss.

ELLIOT: John can be such an ass.

NATALIE: He always was the spontaneous one.

ELLIOT: I had such a crush on him.

NATALIE: You and everyone else... Don't worry, John's probably got it all wrong. The guy'll be some frat boy who's into blonds with big tits.

ELLIOT: Maria Schneider.

NATALIE: Maria Schneider!

JOHN: *(From offstage)* Come on in.

NATALIE: Oh, shit.

(NATALIE grabs the volumes of Das Kapital from the coffee table and tucks them away in the shelves. John enters followed by MARK COLVIN. 30 years-old, handsome, in a corporate suit, He's freshly showered, carrying a backpack with gym towel.)

JOHN: Everyone, this is Mark. Mark, my wife Natalie.

NATALIE: Welcome.

MARK: Thanks for inviting me.

NATALIE: Of course.

(MARK and NATALIE shake hands.)

JOHN: And our old friend, Elliot. Elliot Murphy.

(ELLIOT and MARK shake hands.)

NATALIE: Elliot lives in L A.

ELLIOT: Hopefully, you won't hold it against me.

MARK: My sister and brother-in-law live there.

NATALIE: John, get him a drink.

JOHN: What's your fancy?

MARK: A beer would be good.

(The others freeze.)

NATALIE: ...We're trying one of John's "essential Burgundys".

ELLIOT: Very essential.

MARK: *(To* JOHN*)* ...the essential burgundy. Please.

JOHN: Excellent choice. *(He heads to the wine cabinet and examines the selection.)*

JOHN: We lured Mark over from London.

MARK: I was there with Goldman.

JOHN: Evan spotted you, didn't he?

MARK: He came to speak at Wharton. That's how we met.

JOHN: That's where we find our "best and brightest" ...1976 Penfolds Grange. Perfect.

ELLIOT: We're all old friends from college.

MARK: Really?

NATALIE: We were just talking about how we'd all slept with each other.

JOHN: Sweetie, don't frighten the poor guy.

NATALIE: I'm sorry.

ELLIOT: We did.

MARK: No problem.

*(*JOHN *opens the wine and pours three glasses.)*

JOHN: This is one of the great Australians. And '76 was one of their best. If not the best. You know I met the guys who bought those vineyards. There's a deal I wish we'd brokered.

MARK: The world would probably be a better place if everybody did sleep together.

NATALIE: God forbid.

MARK: Better than if no one slept together.

NATALIE: That'd be a world of religious nuts.

ELLIOT: Called America.

JOHN: You've got some catching up to do.

MARK: I see.

(JOHN *brings over glasses to* ELLIOT *and* MARK.)

NATALIE: What about your wife?... I'm not missing out on the Grange.

JOHN: All right. A tasting on the way.

NATALIE: John says great things about you.

MARK: They've got me on the Georgian project.

JOHN: Our new oil pipeline.

MARK: We're underwriting it.

NATALIE: John got the small landowners a share of the profits. Not easy when you're dealing with Russian Mafioso types.

JOHN: Georgian Mafioso types. One cut below. If that's possible. Drink up.

(They all sip their wine.)

JOHN: So?

ELLIOT: Extraordinary.

MARK: Amazing.

NATALIE: Worth ditching abstinence for.

JOHN: As I said—one of the greats.

(An awkward pause)

MARK: I heard someone at the office say you're a filmmaker?

NATALIE: I make these little movies. Docs. About folks suffering at the hand of capitalism.

MARK: That's a pretty wide range.

NATALIE: I'd say so.

ELLIOT: She's being modest. She's won a Peabody.

JOHN: Two.

ELLIOT: One was about this Inuit community forced to sell their land to some mining company. For nothing. So, they took up painting...now they're world famous.

MARK: *Stone Painters*... I saw it in college. That was yours?

NATALIE: I was dying to call it *Stoned Painters*. But that would have been the death of it on public television.

MARK: It blew me away. It was the first time I'd come face to face with any type of ethnographic art... What are you working on now?

JOHN: She's finishing a documentary on Rwanda.

MARK: You were in Rwanda?

NATALIE: Ten years ago.

JOHN: At the height of the genocide.

MARK: Amazing.

NATALIE: I'm afraid it wasn't "amazing". It was terrible. Unbelievably so. And I could do nothing about it. They still need water. Blood. The most basic necessities.

JOHN: The footage is devastating.

NATALIE: It's phony, if truth be told.

ELLIOT: I'd like to see it.

JOHN: She's having a bit of an artistic crisis.

MARK: I'm sorry.

(NATALIE *gets up and, picking up the Penfolds Grange, tops off her glass.*)

NATALIE: The real reason I'm discouraged is—well it's me. For the first time in my life, I don't know how to make something—something that hits home. Forces an audience to get up and do something. We were talking about it before: how difficult it's become to have any impact.

MARK: I'm sure.

NATALIE: All I see is the complexity...I can't hear the argument, my voice. Does that make sense? Tell me it does.

MARK: Of course.

(JOHN *picks up the Grange and tops up* ELLIOT's *glass.*)

JOHN: How to be meaningful in a country where the superficial's become God?

ELLIOT: Especially at our age.

JOHN: *(To* ELLIOT*)* Your age.

NATALIE: Elliot's the real activist. He's campaigning to help Muhammad Araka. To get him a fair trial.

MARK: You're talking about that guy they arrested in Florida?

NATALIE: On trumped up charges.

ELLIOT: A total frame-up.

NATALIE: We knew him in college.

JOHN: We did.

NATALIE: We were compadres.

ELLIOT: That's how we all met. Politics.

JOHN: True.

MARK: Really?

NATALIE: *(Toasting)* The good old days.

ELLIOT: *(Toasting)* The good old days.

JOHN: Honey...I think...maybe the kitchen?

NATALIE: Of course. You're right. Would you excuse us?

ELLIOT: Do you want a hand?

JOHN: No.

NATALIE: We were going to eat in here on trays. *(To Mark)* Since you're one of the ten people who actually saw *Stone Painters*, you're going to stay I hope?

MARK: Thank you.

NATALIE: We'll use the dining room.

JOHN: We won't be a minute.

NATALIE: Tonight's all about having fun, do you hear?

(JOHN and NATALIE exit. She darts back in with her glass.)

NATALIE: I'm not going without this.

JOHN: *(From offstage)* Natalie.

(NATALIE tops off her glass and exits.)

ELLIOT: They're very into their food.

MARK: Good... Good for us, I guess... *(An uncomfortable pause)* Sounds like you guys did some crazy stuff.

ELLIOT: It wasn't much. To be honest. In the scheme of things.

MARK: That Muslim guy was a Black Panther, wasn't he?

ELLIOT: Yes. This is good, isn't it? Penfolds Grange.

MARK: It's not as though you still believe in all that?

ELLIOT: No... Of course not.

MARK: Good. It's a little...well, it's all kind of out-of-date sounding now, don't you think?

ELLIOT: Spoken like that, I guess you're right... I have to remember that... Sometimes—when I'm not thinking, I hear myself up and telling someone "I'm a practicing Marxist."

MARK: "A practicing Marxist"?

ELLIOT: I know.

MARK: Would you mind if I asked what that actually means?

ELLIOT: Seriously?

MARK: Please.

ELLIOT: Well, Okay...it's been a while since... Okay, Marxists believe that the means of production—all the companies and government enterprises in the world—should be owned by everyone. Especially those who work in them. And that that—shared economic wealth—is the true basis of equality...

MARK: Hm.

ELLIOT: Yeah.

MARK: Sounded good on paper, I'm sure.

ELLIOT: That's about as far as they got. We're still working on it... Did you know John has a sommelier?

MARK: A good one, I hear. He's always talking about him at the office.

ELLIOT: Not a practicing Marxist, that's for sure... And he's straight.

(ELLIOT *and* MARK *sip their wine.*)

MARK: This is not some sort of... you know.

ELLIOT: What?

MARK: Forget it. I'm sorry.

ELLIOT: A set-up? Is that what you're worried about? No, I don't think so. I mean, I hope not. I mean, no, it's not.

MARK: I like to be clear about these things.

ELLIOT: If it makes you feel any better the first thing I knew about it was ten minutes ago.

MARK: Oh, okay.

ELLIOT: I haven't actually seen Natalie and John for three years. They're always going off to Europe. Somehow they never make it to L A. I'm only here because of Muhammad.

MARK: Elliot?

ELLIOT: Yes?

MARK: Look, full disclosure...I think this Muhammad guy deserves what he's got coming to him.

ELLIOT: I'm sorry?

MARK: He's a self-proclaimed Muslim fanatic.

ELLIOT: He's a Muslim, but he's not a fanatic. There's a difference between fanaticism and activism, you know.

MARK: Go on.

ELLIOT: And naturally he's a Muslim. He's taken up a cause embraced by millions of oppressed, poor people around the world. Millions of Americans, too. They're trying to get their fair share. That's all. And religion's a way of building a coalition to do that.

MARK: You don't support those Arab terrorists blowing up innocent people?

ELLIOT: No.

MARK: Good.

ELLIOT: Muhammad is not a terrorist.

MARK: You know what I really hate about all those people is they sound so fucking self righteous all the time.

ELLIOT: Struggling against capitalism and racism can do that to you. They're talking about their political beliefs.

MARK: And that automatically makes you self-righteous?

ELLIOT: No, it makes you define your politics. So you fucking talk about them.

(NATALIE enters, her glass in hand.)

NATALIE: Elliot's been looking after you?

ELLIOT: I'm trying.

MARK: He's doing a great job. Thank you.

NATALIE: The chef's in urgent need of a refill. *(She pours herself a glass of wine.)*

MARK: I really like your apartment.

NATALIE: Thank you.

MARK: *(Off art on mantle)* That's a beautiful...

(MARK heads to the mantle to see exactly what's he complimenting.)

ELLIOT: I love that you still have that photo of Castro.

NATALIE: Of course.

(They both look at the photo and toast. NATALIE sits.)

NATALIE: I'm worried about what's happening to Muhammad. I...I saw him a few years ago. Did I tell you?

ELLIOT: No, you didn't. Where?

NATALIE: We... At the airport. In Madrid. He was on his way to a conference. We talked. I had coffee. We... It was all very matter of fact. *(To MARK)* Excuse us.

MARK: Please.

NATALIE: He didn't tell you about that?

ELLIOT: No, he didn't.

(JOHN *enters.*)

JOHN: Honey, where's my Grange?

NATALIE: Oh, sorry, sweetie.

(JOHN *sees the now empty bottle and heads to the wine cabinet.*)

JOHN: It is really something, isn't it?

ELLIOT: Everything anyone could ask for.

MARK: It's good. Thank you, John.

(JOHN *selects another bottle. Something he obviously likes. And brings out fresh glasses*)

JOHN: So what've I been missing?

NATALIE: Elliot ran into Muhammad last year.

JOHN: Oh, how was he?

ELLIOT: Angry. Bursting with ideas.

JOHN: As a rule Muslims aren't that thrilled about gays. But he likes Elliot.

NATALIE: John, Elliot's one of us.

JOHN: I'm talking about those gay politicos who got murdered in Holland. (*He opens the new bottle and starts pouring.*)

ELLIOT: We're not going to let that happen in America.

JOHN: They don't make 'em like this guy any more.

NATALIE: I wish they did though, don't you?

MARK: Yes...of course.

(JOHN *gestures to the glasses of the new wine.*)

JOHN: How about a little Margaux?

NATALIE: This is so good, John.

JOHN: Honey, go easy.

NATALIE: I'm taking medication.

JOHN: Sweetie...

NATALIE: For my depression.

JOHN: Poor Mark.

(JOHN *passes glasses of Margaux to* ELLIOT *and* MARK.)

NATALIE: He might as well know, too. The experts say it stems from an absence of love. That you haven't adjusted to. A sudden absence usually...John's theory is it's because I'm not working. That I'm not finishing my film.

JOHN: Bottom line is we don't know. And I wish we did.

(JOHN *hands* NATALIE *a small glass of the Margaux.)*

NATALIE: I think we should explain who we are.

JOHN: What on earth are you talking about?

NATALIE: Elliot said we were friends because of politics...

JOHN: So?

NATALIE: Mark doesn't know what that means. Nobody does anymore.

JOHN: I'm sure Mark has a good idea.

ELLIOT: I'm not so sure.

NATALIE: Honey, I'm not having Mark feel like he's being left out.

JOHN: It's too much to ask you to follow doctor's orders?

MARK: It's all right. I'm interested.

NATALIE: Of course you are.

JOHN: You're to blame, you know.

ELLIOT: Me?

NATALIE: So, Mark... Most of what everyone knows about back then are the silly sayings. The T-shirt slogans...

JOHN: "What if they gave a war and nobody came?"

ELLIOT: "War is not healthy for children and other living things"

JOHN: "War is good for business. Invest your son".

ELLIOT: "One Two, Three, Four...We don't want your fucking war."

NATALIE: Guys, guys, please... I'm explaining something to Mark... The thing is, by the time we got to Berkeley, the People's Park, Haight Ashbury was over. We weren't so naïve any more. *(To* ELLIOT*)* I think I'm right, don't you?

ELLIOT: Always.

NATALIE: But there was one thing we did nail down. Applying our politics to our personal relationships.

ELLIOT: Which we owe a lot of to the Women's Movement.

NATALIE: We said we would live and love according to our politics... As friends... And as lovers. We would see each other as equals.

ELLIOT: That's right.

JOHN: Yes.

NATALIE: We were free to see other people. That might seem clichéd now but it wasn't... And it's not. It did mean working on things like, how to wipe out jealousy... which is just insecurity. Possessiveness. *(To* ELLIOT*)* I'm good at this, you know.

ELLIOT: You're great at it.

JOHN: Don't encourage her.

NATALIE: Actually that was just a small part of it, Mark. We made a real commitment to having relationships based on a shared worldview. That's how we would build our lives together.

ELLIOT: She's completely right.

JOHN: Elliot.

NATALIE: It is the thing that separates us from our parents—from all the so-called radicals who came before us. Look at Karl Marx. His wife packed him off to the museum every day. Didn't want to know him. Didn't know what he was writing. Stalin. Our friend, Castro. Mao. Che. Same thing. They simply screwed whoever was in front of them.

JOHN: Any woman that said "no" was taken away and shot.

ELLIOT: End of relationship.

NATALIE: On to the next one. *(To MARK)* The point is, none of them brought their ideas home to their partners.

ELLIOT: Here, here.

NATALIE: It's the one thing I'll take to my grave. The one thing. Everything else's been compromised. But not that.

JOHN: Honey...

NATALIE: Never.

JOHN: We're having a dinner party.

NATALIE: It's the reason we have better marriages. Better relationships. You know, John and I've been together for nearly thirty years.

MARK: It all sounds very...

ELLIOT: "It ain't a free country if you can't smoke what cha'wanna."

JOHN: *(Off his glass)* I'm not so sure about this. Time to break out a Cheval Blanc, I think. *(He takes a bottle of Cheval Blanc from the wine cabinet and proceeds to open it.)*

NATALIE: Cheval Blanc? In the name of John's Cheval Blanc, I'll get off my soapbox. But, I'm right, you know.

MARK: I'm sure you are.

JOHN: This is not only one of the most sought-after wines in the world, but, in my opinion, one of the best.

NATALIE: We brought it back from the Dordogne, didn't we?

JOHN: Yes. You think she might remember.

NATALIE: We rented this *"petit chateau"* last summer.

JOHN: Two summers ago.

NATALIE: I love my husband, Mark.

JOHN: Sweetie. *(He pours three glasses of Cheval Blanc.)*

NATALIE: I'll tell you another thing I'll take to my grave—you can't change the world sober.

JOHN: Who wants to do anything sober?

ELLIOT: Anything?

NATALIE: Not Elliot, that's for sure.

ELLIOT: Give me a glass of that Cheval Blanc, John.

JOHN: It could be dangerous.

ELLIOT: I want it.

JOHN: Coming right up.

(JOHN delivers the Cheval Blanc to ELLIOT and MARK.)

NATALIE: Hey...what about equality? Weren't you listening?

JOHN: I always listen to you, dear. *(He pours one more glass of the Cheval Blanc.)*

NATALIE: Mark, you've been so polite. I know people don't usually go on about Marx, or Mao or anything progressive any more.

JOHN: Honey, shouldn't we be thinking about eating...?

(JOHN hands NATALIE her glass of Cheval Blanc.)

NATALIE: *(Jumping up)* Oh!

JOHN: This is hardly a dinner that cooks itself.

NATALIE: Speaking of things you ought to do sober! *(She runs off with her glass.)*

JOHN: She'll be a minute. I'm going to open one more and let it breath. Just for us guys.

ELLIOT: Us guys.

(JOHN gets another bottle Cheval Blanc out of the wine cabinet.)

JOHN: It's really something, isn't it?

MARK: Yes. Strong.

JOHN: Robust's the term they want us using.

ELLIOT: I'll go for robust.

JOHN: He always goes for robust.

ELLIOT: Thank you, John.

(JOHN opens the wine.)

JOHN: You surviving?

MARK: Oh yes. Thank you. Yes.

JOHN: You?

ELLIOT: I'm drinking myself into survival mode.

JOHN: You've given up changing the world?

ELLIOT: Temporarily.

MARK: Would you mind if I asked you a question?

JOHN: Please. Ask away.

MARK: Back then, did you, young people, actually think you were running the country? Did you?

JOHN: We thought we were.

ELLIOT: We were. As much as you could with Nixon and his fucking goons staring down at you.

JOHN: We did talk all the time about "Revolution".

ELLIOT: Yeah. "Revolution!"

JOHN: All I wanted to do was bomb police stations. R O T C offices, the Pentagon... I thought that was the answer.

ELLIOT: Always the showboater.

JOHN: Thank you.

MARK: Did you know how to make a bomb?

JOHN: It's not that hard.

ELLIOT: You didn't have the first clue. It was a pick-up line.

JOHN: A great pick-up line.

(JOHN *and* ELLIOT *toast.*)

JOHN: You must have done some crazy things.

MARK: Nothing like what you guys did.

JOHN: I guess it's a little harder in this age of total economic rationality.

MARK: I wish it was total. John's philosophy is that no one makes money until you know everything about a country. Its financial system, population make-up. It's the facts that make money.

JOHN: *Das Kapital*. Volume 2. Page 240.

(ELLIOT *goes over and picks up Das Kapital Volume 2 from the shelf where* NATALIE *left it. He flicks through it.*)

MARK: No one actually thinks about the real world. Everyone's got some dream, some plan... But they don't know what's actually going on. That's why we're so successful.

JOHN: You know what? I think Mark needs a bomb in his office.

ELLIOT: Leave that to me. I'll find a rational argument for it.

JOHN: Hey, we're just having fun... Here, take off your jacket. You're here to enjoy yourself... Drink up. (*He tops off* MARK*'s glass.*) If you want to know a dirty little secret, that's really what we did back then: have a fucking blast. And we did, didn't we, Elliot?

ELLIOT: Absolutely.

JOHN: So no holding back. Understand? Not with this crowd.

MARK: All right. "Power to the people."

ELLIOT: Okay.

ELLIOT & JOHN: "Power to the people."

(NATALIE *enters.*)

NATALIE: "Power to the People"?

(ELLIOT *slams Volume 2 of* Das Kapital *closed.*)

ELLIOT: Fuck.

JOHN: Page 240. Am I right?

ELLIOT: Yes.

NATALIE: Before I forget, the checkbook. (*She heads to the desk.*)

ELLIOT: Thank you, Natalie.

NATALIE: I was thinking twenty-five thousand.

ELLIOT: That's very generous.

NATALIE: *(Searching)* There should be one in here...

JOHN: It's in the kitchen, honey.

NATALIE: It used to be in this drawer. *(She closes the desk drawer.)* You know, I think we're the last generation to have real political passion.

ELLIOT: Don't say that.

NATALIE: We are. What's anybody passionate about today?

MARK: We have passion.

NATALIE: What for? Money?

JOHN: Sweetie.

NATALIE: Sorry. I'm sure you have lots of passion.

MARK: You don't really know us.

NATALIE: I probably don't, you're right.

ELLIOT: Personally, I think your generation has a long way to go on the passion front.

MARK: We have amazing passion. For music. Having a good time.

ELLIOT: Having a good time?

MARK: Yeah. Dancing. The internet.

JOHN & NATALIE: The internet?

JOHN: Chat-rooms?

NATALIE: Mark, that's absurd. Passion by its very definition requires a human connection.

JOHN: Natalie, sweetie...

NATALIE: I shouldn't have started drinking, I know. I put a cease and desist order on myself and I slipped up.

JOHN: We'll be eating soon. I promise.

ELLIOT: Good. Can't wait.

MARK: Great.

NATALIE: Mark. I'd like to see some of that passion! You said dancing, didn't you?

MARK: ...Uh...

JOHN: Honey.

NATALIE: You're lucky. You happened to catch me in a mood.

JOHN: Natalie, please.

NATALIE: You better have some good moves, buddy. "Passionate" ones.

JOHN: You don't have to.

ELLIOT: Of course, he does.

(NATALIE *turns on the music and goes over to* MARK. *He stands there: nervous, frozen. She clears away the chair in front of him and begins dancing...*MARK *takes a deep breath.*)

MARK: Okay. (*He does a few uptight dance moves.*)

NATALIE: C'mon... You can do better than that.

(NATALIE *pulls* MARK *into the middle of the room and gets into a real groove. He gradually lifts his game. And very soon matches her. He's good. Much more than good as she discovers—to her delight.* JOHN *and* ELLIOT *watch. The dancing gets increasingly wild, positively risque. After a while* NATALIE *and* MARK *lose momentum and stagger to a halt.*)

NATALIE: (*Excited*) All right... A round of applause for Mark.

(*The guys clap.*)

ELLIOT & JOHN: Bravo! Bravo!

(NATALIE *turns off the music.*)

NATALIE: *(Out of breath)* I shouldn't've doubted you. I'm sorry.

MARK: No problem...

NATALIE: I stand corrected. He does have passion.

MARK: And we've got great drugs, too. My generation.

NATALIE: You do? What?

ELLIOT: Crystal?

NATALIE: Crystal? What does crystal do?

ELLIOT: Uh...

JOHN: Go on. Tell us.

MARK: No, it's all right. But we are funny. That's for sure. A lot funnier than you guys...

ALL: Ohhh...

MARK: We are. You don't believe me?

NATALIE: Funnier than Pryor? Carlin...? The real George Carlin?

MARK: Yes.

ELLIOT: Oh, O K. Mister Funny Guy. Tell us a joke.

JOHN: You heard the man.

MARK: All right.

NATALIE: I love this guy. No quitting while he's ahead.

ELLIOT: Why should he? They are so much funnier.

JOHN: The floor is yours, buddy.

MARK: They're kind of over the edge.

ELLIOT: We do have a sense of humor, believe it or not.

MARK: I have a whole bunch of them...

JOHN: Of course, you do.

NATALIE: C'mon. Out with it.

MARK: They all end with the same punch line— "and he was the best little nigger in the world".

NATALIE: "The best little...in the world"?

MARK: Yeah...I'm in this joke club, you know and when I started I thought, shit, this is going to be impossible. But once I got the swing of it, it wasn't. It was pretty easy.

NATALIE: I'm sure it was. *(To JOHN)* Sometimes I wonder why I ever listen to you. *(She gets up.)* We should go in... *(To ELLIOT)* You don't mind waiting a second or two, do you? We need water. I need water. Sparkling. John, it's in the fridge.

JOHN: I'll get it. *(He exits.)*

NATALIE: Do you like risotto, Elliot?

ELLIOT: Yes.

NATALIE: *(To MARK)* Mark?

MARK: Yes.

NATALIE: Good. *(She exits.)*

(ELLIOT gets up, and follows after her. MARK remains.)

END OF ACT ONE

ACT TWO

(After dinner)

*(JOHN enters with open bottles of wine from dinner: a
red, and a white. He gets two fresh glasses out of the wine
cabinet. Sound of a toilet flushing from off-stage. JOHN
pours a glass of red.)*

(A pause)

(MARK enters.)

JOHN: White or red?

MARK: I'm fine, John. Honestly.

JOHN: Try the red. You'll like it.

MARK: Okay.

(JOHN hands the glass of red to MARK. Pours himself one)

JOHN: Sorry about all the politics. I'm afraid with Elliot
here that can't be helped.

MARK: He's very committed.

JOHN: We were young. We didn't know better...
Luckily as you grow older you come to realize it's the
little things—half-assed risottos—that flea-ridden hotel
in the Dordogne Natalie was going on about—that's
what's really important.

MARK: I agree.

JOHN: Last summer we were on this yacht north of
Dubrovnik. One afternoon I was swimming back to the

boat and I look up. And Natalie's asleep on the deck.
This beautiful, beautiful woman. Stunning. And all of
a sudden it felt like that first time all over again... I'm
embarrassing you, I'm sorry.

MARK: No, no.

JOHN: Berkeley Theater. *Tout Va Bien*. I don't even
know why I went... She's incredible, isn't she?

MARK: Yes.

JOHN: You know, I don't hear half the things she says
anymore. I don't need to. After thirty years, you don't.

MARK: It's God's will. A great marriage.

JOHN: You think so?

MARK: That's what my grandmother says.

JOHN: I'm a lucky man, Mark. I am. Someone like your
grandmother'd probably say I'm blessed. But you and
I both know success can evaporate in an instant. That's
why...she and I. No one can take that away from me.

MARK: No.

JOHN: And don't worry about all this brouhaha with
Muhammad. Natalie wants to feel she's still living on
some radical cutting edge...hanging out with angry
friends... The truth is that's what I like that about her. I
liked that about her the day I met her. It's the thing that
truly makes her her.

MARK: I see that.

JOHN: I hate to break to it to you. It's got nothing to do
with God.

MARK: I'd like to feel like that about someone one day.

JOHN: I'm sure you will... You know, anytime you want
to move elsewhere I'd be happy to set it up. Get you
moved up a notch or two.

MARK: Thank you.

JOHN: Not a bad idea now that I think about it.

MARK: What do you mean?

JOHN: Well, I'm a big believer in comfort zones. Particularly at my office.

MARK: John, I love where I am. Honest to God.

JOHN: You're an ambitious guy. Ready for a new challenge.

MARK: You've already done me a big favor. Bringing me over from London.

JOHN: I'm about to do you a bigger favor.

MARK: Is this all because of the joke?

JOHN: I told you. It's a comfort zone thing.

MARK: I don't understand. The joke club's—

JOHN: Careful.

MARK: ...it's mandatory for junior management.

JOHN: It's garbage. Disgusting garbage.

MARK: Evan told me—

JOHN: I'm not interested in what Evan told you. He doesn't speak for me. Nor the firm. Never did. Never will.

MARK: Of course. Sorry.

JOHN: Consider it a done deal, all right?

MARK: All right.

JOHN: That gives me an idea. (*He heads to the wine cabinet. After a search, he finds what he's looking for: definitely not one of his usual suspects.*)

JOHN: Dalmatian Red. Never tried it.

MARK: I'm fine.

JOHN: C'mon, you're only young once. *(He unscrews the wine top and pours two glasses.)* We picked this up on that trip. Dingac Plavak. Their version of a Zin... Here.

MARK: *(Taking a glass)* Thank you.

JOHN: And take my advice, think about swimming back to that boat.

MARK: Okay.

JOHN: Promise me.

MARK: Promise.

JOHN: Good... Cheers.

(They drink. ELLIOT enters.)

ELLIOT: Your wife wants you.

JOHN: Her wish is my command. Elliot, don't you laugh.

NATALIE: *(Off stage)* John.

JOHN: *(To MARK)* Pour the man some of the Plavak.

ELLIOT: Plavak?

(JOHN exits.)

ELLIOT: Good desert.

MARK: Yes.

ELLIOT: The wine was better.

MARK: John was raving about it.

ELLIOT: Who wouldn't? *(He pours a glass of the Plavak.)*

MARK: John…wants me to leave the firm... He's firing me...

ELLIOT: I'm sure John's not doing that.

MARK: He's offered to move me up. In another company.

ELLIOT: Sounds like a good thing.

MARK: You don't understand Wall Street, do you?

ELLIOT: Not to the extent you want any of us to.

MARK: He says they'll "find" me another position. Which they'll do. I'll go over there. We'll have a couple of meetings. See whether I'm the right "fit"... Things will drag on... In a couple of months, word'll come back "This isn't really the right time". And I'm out of a job.

(ELLIOT *tastes the Plavak.*)

ELLIOT: This is interesting.

MARK: I'm being fucking fired. Are you listening to me? ...Do you know where this joke club is?

ELLIOT: I'm not really keen to revisit all that. Sorry.

MARK: Once a month at seven A M. In our conference room on the forty-sixth floor. Everyone in global research is there. You don't have any choice. There are prizes. I won fiteen hundred dollars once...

ELLIOT: Mark—

MARK: There are no blacks at the firm. Why would there be? The whole place runs on economic rationalism. Anything African—you name it—too risky. Not for our clients. John knows about the club. They still tell his jokes. They're legendary.

ELLIOT: John's a great guy.

MARK: I wish I'd never come. I wish I'd never met any of you people.

ELLIOT: I'll take that as a compliment.

MARK: I'm not some racist, you know...

ELLIOT: All right.

MARK: You have no idea what it takes to work at John's firm, do you? The hours. What they ask you to do? Nothing's too stupid, too menial. A partner's dry cleaning? Got it. Walking their girlfriend's dog? Done. Letting my boss's old college buddy come on to me? No problem. Evan telling me how important it is to keep millions and millions of *them* behind bars...? I can't say anything. That's not part of my job.

ELLIOT: No?

MARK: I only had to stick it out another two years. Then I'd've had my pick. I could've gone anywhere. I'd've been made for life. At my age. Do you have any idea...? No, of course you wouldn't.

ELLIOT: Well, if you weren't a racist you might have felt a little guilty, I would have thought... on your meteoric rise to the top.

MARK: What do you think?

ELLIOT: When I come across people like you, I can't even fathom... What do you say when you meet black C F Os, black ambassadors, politicians... Oh, don't bother, what's the point... *(Off the wine)* I like this. When it comes to mood-altering substances, John always has the best.

MARK: Do you know how smug you are?

ELLIOT: I've spent my whole life fighting racism. I think we've come a long way...Blacks, Asians...us. Not far enough. Never far enough... but a long, long way. And I fucking promise you, we'll get there.

(A long pause)

MARK: When I was living in London, I used to date this black guy. Anthony. He'd gone to Oxford. After I got the job here he'd come to visit me... One afternoon we're walking through the Village and I see Evan. I pushed—literally shoved—Anthony down these stairs. I wasn't about to let Evan see us... Anthony was freaked. I told him I didn't want them knowing I was gay. He understood. Didn't like it but understood... Next time we talked he told me he'd met someone else.

ELLIOT: So you liked this Anthony?

MARK: Yes.

ELLIOT: This guy you could tell "best little nigger" jokes about?

MARK: I'm fucked up. All right? *(A pause)* So...Were there a lot of hot guys doing what you were doing? Back then? Sharing the love as it were.

ELLIOT: "Sharing the love"?

MARK: Isn't that how you used to say it?

ELLIOT: I guess so. If you really want to know, they were mostly straight. The ones I liked...

MARK: Okay.

ELLIOT: After I moved to L A, I met—Roger. We were together for over...for a long time.

MARK: But you guys split up?

ELLIOT: Roger died.

MARK: Shit, I'm sorry.

ELLIOT: We tried to split up...I mean we were headed that way. But he got sick, and I'm not built for leaving someone... A lot of people did. Some people did. Leave their lovers. Who could blame them? They... It's been years now. What am I doing? "Practicing Marxists". We're supposed to be masters of discretion...

MARK: It's a pretty good cover.

ELLIOT: What do you mean?

MARK: Helps keep you single.

(ELLIOT and MARK drink.)

MARK: You know what I was thinking about all through dinner?

ELLIOT: No.

MARK: You all talking about everyone doing everything with everyone. The great sex you all had. You especially.

ELLIOT: History does tend to exaggerate.

MARK: I was thinking about what it'd be like to kiss you.

(A pause)

(ELLIOT stands and heads to the wine cabinet.)

MARK: I think I'm right. You are hiding behind all this "I only kiss Marxists" crap.

(ELLIOT grabs the first bottle he can put his hands on. Without looking at the label, he proceeds to open it.)

ELLIOT: How old are you?

MARK: What's it to you?

ELLIOT: Just asking.

MARK: Did you hear what I just said?

ELLIOT: Who said anything about my being single? *(He opens the bottle.)* All right, I probably do hide behind it...I'm scared...if you really want to know.

MARK: You have so much going for you.

ELLIOT: I'll pretend I didn't hear that. *(He sits down and takes a sip.)* This is strong.

MARK: It's probably from the Dordogne.

ELLIOT: If I have to hear another fucking word about the fucking Dordogne.

(ELLIOT and MARK laugh. NATALIE enters.)

NATALIE: You're doing all right in here?... *(Eyeing the wine)* d'Yquem! John brought out the d'Yquem? No wonder you're laughing! *(She runs to get a glass and holds it out to* ELLIOT.) Do you know how expensive this is? Pour me some...

(ELLIOT *pours.)*

ELLIOT: We love the d'Yquem.

MARK: Er... Yes!

NATALIE: Cheers!

ELLIOT & MARK: Cheers!

(They drink.)

ELLIOT: Great.

NATALIE: I'm sorry about the risotto.

ELLIOT: What are you talking about? It was great.

MARK: Delicious, I thought.

NATALIE: The secret is not putting the scallops in until the last minute. John had the whole thing explained to him in Bologna.

MARK: Not the Dordogne?

(ELLIOT *and* MARK *suppress a laugh.)*

NATALIE: What?

ELLIOT: Nothing.

NATALIE: John loves this wine. It's his absolute favorite.

ELLIOT: John wants to relieve Mark of his job.

NATALIE: He does not.

ELLIOT: Well, he says he's going to find him another position...

MARK: I made a mistake. About the joke thing. I'm sorry.

NATALIE: Thank you.

ELLIOT: He had a black boyfriend.

NATALIE: You don't need to say that. *(A pause)* I hate it when things don't turn out right. It's not that difficult, you know. If you just watch over it and keep stirring. *(She takes a sip of d'Yquem.)*

NATALIE: Did you know that the oldest written expression in the Polish language is about risotto? "Giveth to me, I shall stir and you shall rest."

ELLIOT: Hmm.

MARK: Yes.

(JOHN enters.)

NATALIE: Sweetie! You opened the d'Yquem!

(JOHN sees the nearly empty wine bottle, goes to the wine cabinet, and retrieves another bottle of d'Yquem.)

JOHN: Jesus, you have to be quick around here.

NATALIE: You have to give John his due. No fuss. no fanfare. Simply the best.

JOHN: Of course.

NATALIE: I mean, who can stand those pompous asses who go on and on about—this bouquet, that aftertaste... Haven't they ever had a whopping hangover? That's what I want to know.

JOHN: According to Thomas Jefferson it's the best sweet wine France ever produced...

NATALIE: Thank you, T J.

(JOHN pours himself a glass of d'Yquem.)

JOHN: Joe Stalin loved its unctuous, sweet taste. I'm not kidding. You know Sotheby's auctioned off some of his collection last year. Wish I'd bought some. That'd be a deal clincher in Georgia.

NATALIE: To the Gulag! Come on everybody.

ALL: To the Gulag!

NATALIE: Once more to the Gulag!

ALL: The Gulag!

(JOHN, *fresh bottle in hand, sits.*)

JOHN: The secret to victory is never running low on ammunition.

ELLIOT: You should send a bottle to Muhammad.

JOHN: I should. You can bet your life this is what all good terrorists aspire to.

NATALIE: I was surprised he'd put on so much weight.

ELLIOT: It suits him.

NATALIE: I was scared to death when I first laid eyes on him in Berkeley. God, I wanted him.

JOHN: You wanted everybody.

NATALIE: So did you.

JOHN: I wanted you, sweetie.

NATALIE: I know.

MARK: What about Elliot in the wanting department?

NATALIE: His time came later.

JOHN: When they all came raging out of the closet, and fucked themselves stupid.

NATALIE: John.

JOHN: What? He's proud of it. So are we for that matter.

NATALIE: Elliot never had so much sex in his life... One day he calls and says he hasn't been laid in forty-eight hours. He was about to slash his wrists.

ELLIOT: Natalie, for God's sake.

NATALIE: He had this accountant in Santa Monica who only took on clients who were sex buddies...he spaced them out over the day... Decades and decades of orgasms compressed into three or four years.

MARK: *(To* ELLIOT*)* Were you into..? I mean... Were you into leather?

ELLIOT: I beg your pardon?

JOHN: He was an accountant.

ELLIOT: John.

MARK: You did say you did everything.

ELLIOT: *They* said I did everything. We didn't believe in the commodification of sex. Fetishes are fun but ultimately they're heartless. A perfect example of how capitalism turns everything human into a product.

JOHN: He was into leather.

ELLIOT: You know this from Marx, John.

JOHN: Chaps.

NATALIE: It was all about quantity back then.

ELLIOT: All right. I admit it, I had a lot of sex... And it was twenty-four hours!

MARK: Good.

NATALIE: I'm proposing a toast. To thirty years of sex.

ELLIOT: Thirty years of sex.

JOHN: Thirty years of sex.

MARK: A hundred years of sex.

NATALIE: Good luck.

(They drink.)

NATALIE: *(To* ELLIOT*)* I wish you would find someone compatible.

ELLIOT & JOHN: Natalie.

NATALIE: I'm serious...how hard can it be?

ELLIOT: It's like a crusade with them.

NATALIE: You know what I'm talking about. Just because he's a progressive doesn't mean he can't find someone.

JOHN: A progressive, liberal, Marxist, fetishist, revolutionary.

ELLIOT: Mark knows what you mean. I'm sure.

MARK: I do.

NATALIE: Is this it with the d'Yquem?

JOHN: What do you think?

NATALIE: There has to be more!

JOHN: At a thousand dollars a bottle? Of course there is.

ELLIOT: No.

JOHN: What do we care? Capitalism provides for all. *(He exits.)*

NATALIE: I told you it'd be like old times, didn't I?

ELLIOT: Right now I can't remember.

MARK: I might just excuse myself for a moment. *(He heads to the small door he came out of at the beginning of the act.)*

NATALIE: There's a nicer one down the hall.

(MARK retraces his steps and exits out the entrance hallway.)

NATALIE: We owe you a big apology.

ELLIOT: He's not so bad.

NATALIE: You're so fucking male.

ELLIOT: So?

NATALIE: Fine. He's gay. You're excused...

ELLIOT: He is kind of hot.

NATALIE: For God's sake.

ELLIOT: And he likes me.

NATALIE: That's why I hate minority politics. The moment they sign you up—the fucking women's movement, black movement, whatever—it and everything in it becomes God. Screw the rest of us.

ELLIOT: He's not as racist as you think.

NATALIE: Elliot, please.

ELLIOT: The joke club he's in is at the office.

NATALIE: Stop defending him.

ELLIOT: It goes on every week. Prizes are given out. And John... They still tell his jokes.

NATALIE: I don't know anything about it.

ELLIOT: You do know there are no blacks at the firm?

NATALIE: Mark told you this?

ELLIOT: Yes.

NATALIE: You're drunk, Elliot. He's coming on to you.

ELLIOT: Thank you.

NATALIE: John's a huge success in a thoroughly venal world. I don't ask him what he does. It's the last thing he wants to talk about when he comes home.

ELLIOT: All right.

NATALIE: He's John, remember? Our John.

ELLIOT: I know.

(JOHN *enters. A bottle of d'Yquem in each hand.*)

JOHN: Ta da!

NATALIE: Mark's been telling Elliot what a racist place your office is.

JOHN: He's not holding back, is he? Did he tell you what we're called on the street?

ELLIOT: No.

JOHN: He left out "The White Supremacy Channel".

NATALIE: I don't like the sound of that.

JOHN: That's the whole point.

ELLIOT: What does go on down there?

JOHN: You want me to explain it to you?

ELLIOT: If you wouldn't mind.

JOHN: I don't mind... We've been damn lucky over the last ten years. First the Russians, then the Georgians. Now the outliers. They've made us a fortune... You'll die when you hear what I tell them. That like them I was a Communist once. I quote a line or two from *The Communist Manifesto*. That gets a big laugh and we're in the door. And thanks to all the oil these folks have, we've done well. Very, very well...I told you, Elliot, *Das Kapital* reading group.

ELLIOT: You're saying there is no joke club?

JOHN: Elliot, success comes with a price. Your competitors get jealous. They start playing dirty. Look at all those discrimination suits. You think women file that stuff without someone paying them? With us it's the rumor treatment. Competitors spreading lies. The kind of trumped-up racist crap little Meth Head's been going on about. But what can you do? Nothing. You learn to ignore it and we tell our employees to do the same. And that's exactly what we should be doing here.

NATALIE: All business is racist when you come right down to it...I don't know how people do what John does.

JOHN: It's not for the Peabody crowd, we all know that.

(MARK *enters.*)

MARK: I should be going.

NATALIE: My husband's opened another bottle of d'Yquem.

ELLIOT: One more glass.

MARK: I don't...

ELLIOT: Pour him some more, John.

(JOHN *goes to get* MARK *a fresh glass.*)

JOHN: We're running out of glasses.

NATALIE: We can't be. *(She runs to the small hall and returns with more wine glasses. Cheap ones)*

JOHN: *(Handing* MARK *a glass)* Sit...sit.

ELLIOT: John's been explaining why people say those things about the office. I was defending you.

JOHN: Just correcting the record. No harm, no foul. Honey, did you tell Elliot about our anniversary party?

NATALIE: No!

JOHN: We're taking all of our friends to Morocco.

NATALIE: You're invited, Elliot.

ELLIOT: Oh, thanks.

NATALIE: You get to bring someone.

MARK: Muhammad?

JOHN: I don't think that'll be happening.

MARK: He was an old friend of yours from college, wasn't he?

JOHN: So?

NATALIE: He was joking, sweetie.

ELLIOT: Actually, I think he's making a larger point, John.

JOHN: Were you?

ELLIOT: Yes, he was.

JOHN: Really? What?

NATALIE: Honey, for God's sake.

JOHN: What was your point, Mark?

ELLIOT: You know exactly what it was.

(A pause)

JOHN: We have a history with Muhammad, Mark. In case you didn't know.

MARK: I didn't know.

JOHN: *(To* ELLIOT*)* Has she told you about her little jaunts over the years?

ELLIOT: What do you mean?

NATALIE: I don't imagine I have.

JOHN: All the emergency trips. Late night phone calls asking for money. Legal advice—everything Muhammad wants now. All very pious. Except—they got it on. *(A pause)* Honey?

NATALIE: We did.

JOHN: I'm not supposed to say anything. Good leftists don't. Jealousy's "bourgeois". Love can't be tainted by possessiveness... It has to be free-floating, spontaneous...

NATALIE: John has to be possessive. Surprise.

JOHN: After thirty years, I'd say I've earned the right.

NATALIE: I'd say so.

JOHN: *(To* MARK*)* So, now you understand why I don't appreciate your addition to my guest list.

NATALIE: When John gets drunk he tends to get all sensitive.

JOHN: And less interested in being polite. As far as I know, Elliot, it's still going on.

NATALIE: Now you're being absurd.

JOHN: I would like to think I am. *(To* ELLIOT*)* Muhammad asked you to come, didn't he? He knew she wouldn't be able to refuse him.

ELLIOT: I haven't spoken to him in a year.

JOHN: Sure.

NATALIE: Believe me, we would support him even if we didn't know him. He's an example to us all.

JOHN: He was a loser when we knew him. And he still is.

NATALIE: He's an actual revolutionary.

JOHN: He's an asshole you're still sleeping with.

NATALIE: It is possible that someone can have revolutionary politics and not sleep with me.

JOHN: Really?

ELLIOT: I think that's enough, don't you?

NATALIE: I'm sorry.

JOHN: You slept with him in Madrid. Three years ago. On your way back from Kinshasa.

NATALIE: I know you're having a bad night, John.

JOHN: I spoke to the hotel manager.

NATALIE: You spoke to the hotel manager?

JOHN: Muhammad was with you.

NATALIE: He was on his way to a conference in Mannheim. We met at the airport and yes, we talked. Of course we did.

JOHN: You slept together. I spoke to the hotel manager.

NATALIE: All right, if it makes you feel better, we did.

ELLIOT: Natalie.

NATALIE: I'm proud of it.

ELLIOT: She's drunk.

NATALIE: Obviously not drunk enough. Anyway, it's finished. Done. Over.

JOHN: Why would I believe that?

NATALIE: Well, for one thing he's in jail... Pass me the d'Yquem.

ELLIOT: Natalie...

JOHN: If she wants to make a complete fool of herself...

(JOHN *hands* NATALIE *the d'Yquem.*)

JOHN: You lied to me about Madrid.

NATALIE: I simply didn't tell you.

JOHN: You've been lying to me for years.

NATALIE: I'd love to know when you turned so fucking bourgeois.

JOHN: I believe it was the moment you got in bed with that fat nigger.

NATALIE: John.

JOHN: He belongs behind bars. They all do.

ELLIOT: John!

JOHN: He's an animal. Niggers are animals.

ELLIOT: Stop.

JOHN: Don't get all pious on us, for Christ's sake. This one tells nigger jokes...and you...how many black friends do you have?

ELLIOT: Plenty, thank you. I work with them every day.

JOHN: When you have a dinner party... how many blacks are there? None. Stand up and be honest for once.

ELLIOT: What has happened to you?

JOHN: What the fuck do you think?

NATALIE: *(To* MARK*)* Everything you told Elliot about the office is true, isn't it?

JOHN: I've built a business out of it. That's why we get to drink this. Happy now?

NATALIE: You want to know why I didn't tell you about Madrid?

JOHN: You're depressed? You're medicated? You're in a fucking stupor?

NATALIE: No, I was scared I'd find out that you and I no longer share the things that really matter. That have to matter.

JOHN: Open relationships? That's what you're talking about?

NATALIE: You know exactly what I'm talking about.

JOHN: You were too busy running off to Long Dong Silver to understand what we do share.

ELLIOT: John...buddy. Please.

JOHN: Shut up.

NATALIE: I don't think shit-faced drunk's going to be good enough.

JOHN: But you're right about one thing. Absolutely fucking right... We have nothing in common. Absolutely nothing.

NATALIE: I wish we did have drugs.

JOHN: You're awash with drugs...I need some whisky.

NATALIE: That's not what you need.

JOHN: You have no idea what I need. And even if you did, you wouldn't give it to me... We've barely touched each other in years.

NATALIE: Why on earth would we?

JOHN: That's a good fucking question. *(He exits.)*

(A long agonizing pause)

NATALIE: ...More d'Yquem?

MARK: No, thank you.

NATALIE: I can't tell my shrink...shrinks. John pays their bills. You heard what he did with that hotel manager.

ELLIOT: I'm so sorry.

NATALIE: It's been going on forever.

ELLIOT: Natalie...

NATALIE: This... Him. After we left Berkeley and moved here. John gave up pot and turned to wine. He'd make jokes about my being the family socialist. The card-carrying member of the "free love and disease crowd". He loved that expression. It became his way of attacking me. Attacking everything I believed in... But I didn't know the half of it, did I? *(She slowly sips her wine.)*

NATALIE: You understand why I have to see Muhammad, don't you?

ELLIOT: Yes.

NATALIE: Mark?

MARK: Yes.

NATALIE: I can truly love him.

MARK: Of course.

NATALIE: Elliot, it's not a fucking "absence of love". There never was any love to begin with.

ELLIOT: Of course there was.

NATALIE: There can't have been. *(A long pause)* It's fine if you want to leave.

ELLIOT: No.

NATALIE: Why don't you go out for a drink?

ELLIOT: Not now.

NATALIE: It's a good idea. Why not?

ELLIOT: It's not a good time.

NATALIE: It's never a good time for you. Why is that?

ELLIOT: Natalie.

MARK: I know this place over on Amsterdam.

(JOHN *enters carrying an open bottle of whisky.*)

JOHN: Glenmorangie...

NATALIE: Give it here.

JOHN: ..."Twenty-five years to the day." "Handcrafted by the Sixteen Men of Tain."

(JOHN *hands* NATALIE *the Glenmorangie. She pours some into one of the cheap wine glasses.*)

JOHN: She has to have it in a glass. That's what they do in Madrid. Drink whisky from a glass.

NATALIE: They're hitting it off. These two.

JOHN: They are? All right. Let's drink a toast. Long time since he was a "sex machine", you know.

NATALIE: Shut up, John.

JOHN: *(To* ELLIOTT*)* Congratulations. Found yourself a closet liberal. *(To* MARK*)* Make sure he takes you to *The Conformist.*

MARK: I've seen it.

JOHN: It's refreshing to see some sign of libido in this apartment... Makes me believe in... Shit, I don't care. Life after death?

NATALIE: You should go.

JOHN: We're drinking to the happy couple. Elliot's a good guy. A straight-shooter. *(To* NATALIE*)* A straight-shooter. Did you hear me?

NATALIE: Yes, John.

JOHN: Wait, I've got a toast for my wife.

MARK: Let's go.

NATALIE: Please.

JOHN: You're not joining me?

ELLIOT: Let it alone, John.

JOHN: Make me.

*(*ELLIOT *and* JOHN *face off.)*

MARK: Elliot.

ELLIOT: Look, I don't know how to say this...

NATALIE: What?

JOHN: For fuck's sake.

ELLIOT: The Committee.

NATALIE: Of course. *(She stands.)*

JOHN: Sit down.

MARK: Elliot.

ELLIOT: It's why I came.

JOHN: It's why he always comes. It'd be a joke if it wasn't so pathetic.

MARK: It's not pathetic.

JOHN: I said "sit down".

*(*NATALIE *heads to the desk and pulls open the drawer.)*

NATALIE: There is a checkbook here. I saw it the other day.

*(*JOHN *steps over and slams the drawer shut.)*

NATALIE: John.

JOHN: What?

(JOHN *grabs* NATALIE*'s wrist, pulling her away from the desk.*)

NATALIE: You're hurting me.

JOHN: Good.

NATALIE: Fuck you.

JOHN: Sit down.

(NATALIE *sits down.*)

NATALIE: Sorry.

ELLIOT: So am I.

JOHN: A toast. To "open relationships"! (*He takes a swig of whisky.*)

ELLIOT: We should go.

(ELLIOT *and* MARK *head for the hallway.*)

NATALIE: Please don't tell Muhammad.

JOHN: Make sure you mention my name. The firm. The whole nine yards.

NATALIE: Don't say anything, I beg you.

JOHN: "The White Supremacy Channel", don't leave that out.

NATALIE: Do I have to get down on my knees?

JOHN: And the joke club. He'll lap that up.

MARK: (*To* ELLIOT) Come on.

NATALIE: Elliot!

(MARK *puts his hand on* ELLIOT*'s shoulder. They head down the hall.*)

JOHN: Assholes. They are so fucking self-righteous. Homosexuals.

NATALIE: (*To* JOHN) Stop.

(The sound of the hall door closing)

(A long pause)

(NATALIE stares around the room.)

NATALIE: God...look at this place.

(Glasses of all shapes and sizes, many half-empty, along with all the opened bottles, are scattered about the apartment. At first stunned by the wreckage, then gradually taking this and everything else in, NATALIE decides to pick up a glass or two. JOHN watches as she all too slowly places them to one side.)

NATALIE: I wish I knew what happened with the risotto.

JOHN: Risotto's impossible if you're having more than one guest.

NATALIE: It was only supposed to be Elliot. *(She sits down and takes a hefty sip of whisky.)*

NATALIE: They seemed to like it.

JOHN: They were drunk.

NATALIE: That's what explains the risotto.

JOHN: I'm getting you some water. *(He gets up.)*

NATALIE: That kid has sex written all over him.

JOHN: Sex'd be good for Elliot.

NATALIE: You did do it, didn't you?

JOHN: Do what?

NATALIE: With Elliot?

JOHN: What do you think? *(A pause)* I love you, you know that.

NATALIE: No! Don't ever say that to me again. It's not true. I know it's not true...

JOHN: Natalie...

NATALIE: You heard. *(She goes to the cabinet drawer.)* There's a checkbook here. I know there is. *(She finds the check book and pulls it out.)* Fuck. *(Returning to the drawer, she discovers a bottle of pills. She grabs it.)* I want someone to tell Elliot not to talk to Muhammad.

(JOHN watches.)

NATALIE: I can take these, you know. All of them. Any time I like. You're never around. *(She sits down and goes to open them. As she does, the pill bottle flies from her grasp, and falls to the floor, its contents flying everywhere. She drops to the floor and starts picking up the pills.)* If you loved me like you just said you did, you would call Elliot.

JOHN: I'm going to bed. *(He steps into the hall...and turns to look at her.)*

NATALIE: "Waste not, want not." *(She picks up pills off the floor.)*

JOHN: Are you coming? *(He keeps watching.)* I'll call Elliot tomorrow. *(He exits.)*

NATALIE: Thank you, John. *(Realizing he's left. Louder)* Thank you, John.

END OF PLAY